Sea Animals

Siân Smith

 Raintree

Raintree is an imprint of Capstone Global Library Limited, a company incorporated in England and Wales having its registered office at 7 Pilgrim Street, London, EC4V 6LB – Registered company number: 6695582

www.raintreepublishers.co.uk
myorders@raintreepublishers.co.uk

Edited by Sian Smith and Diyan Leake
Designed by Marcus Bell
Picture research by Tracy Cummins
Production by Helen McCreath
Originated by Capstone Global Library Ltd
Printed and bound in China

ISBN 978 1 406 28064 7
18 17 16 15 14
10 9 8 7 6 5 4 3 2 1

British Library Cataloguing in Publication Data
Smith, Sian.
Sea animals. -- (Animal in their habitats)
A full catalogue record for this book is available from the British Library.

Acknowledgements
We would like to thank the following for permission to reproduce photographs: Getty Images pp. 4 (Steven Hunt), 5 (Gerard Soury), 6 (Jeff Rotman), 8 (Reinhard Dirscherl), 11 (Jason Isley – Scubazoo), 15 (Barry Fackler), 18 (Douglas Klug), 22b (Barry Fackler); Shutterstock pp. 7 (Krzysztof Odziomek), 9 (Beth Swanson), 10 (CHEN WS), 12 (Sokolov Alexey), 13 (serg_dibrova), 14 (Andrea Izzotti), 16, 22a (Dray van Beeck), 17 (outdoorsman), 19 (Joost van Uffelen), 20a (Rich Carey), 20b (Potapov Alexander), 20c (Kirsanov Valeriy Vladimirovich), 20d (KAMONRAT), 21 (nitrogenic. com).

Cover photograph of a Green Sea Turtle over a coral reef in Hawaii, USA, reproduced with permission of National Geographic Creative (JAMES FORTE).

Back cover photograph reproduced with permission of Shutterstock (Krzysztof Odziomek).

We would like to thank Michael Bright for his invaluable help in the preparation of this book.

Every effort has been made to contact copyright holders of material reproduced in this book. Any omissions will be rectified in subsequent printings if notice is given to the publisher.

Contents

Animals in the sea

Can you see the octopus?

Can you see the cod?

frogfish

Can you see the frogfish?

Can you see the clown fish?

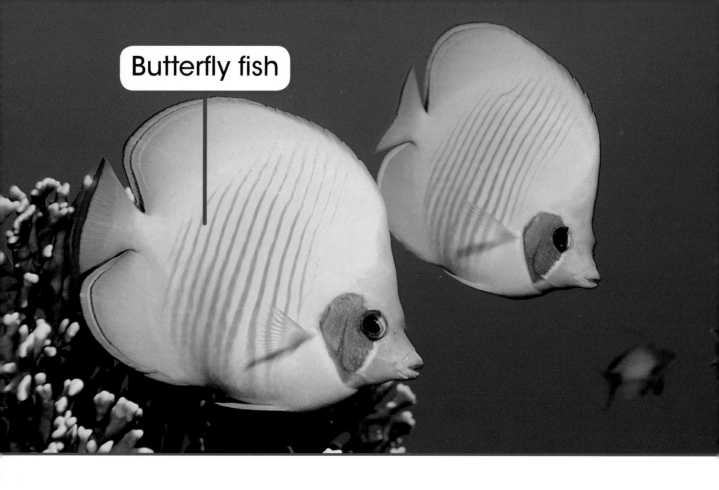

Can you see the butterfly fish?

Can you see the puffer fish?

Can you see the seahorse?

Can you see the sea snake?

Can you see the dolphin?

Can you see the turtle?

Can you see the shark?

Can you see the manta ray?

Can you see the eel?

Can you see the walrus?

Can you see the seal?

Can you see the whale?

Living in the sea

turtle

dolphin

tiger

bat

There are seas all over the world. Water in the sea is salty.

Which of these animals live in the sea?

20

Answer: turtle and dolphin

What am I?

I am a very fast swimmer.

I eat plants and tiny animals.

I look like a flat kite.

The last part of my name rhymes with "day".

Picture glossary

eel

manta ray

Index

Notes for teachers and parents

Before reading

Tuning in: Ask the children if they have ever been to the seaside. Talk about how the seas cover twice as much of the Earth as the land. Many animals live in the sea. Some are mammals.

After reading

Recall and reflection: Which sea animals in the book have fins? (cod, frogfish, clown fish, butterfly fish, puffer fish – although you can't really see its fins in the photograph – seahorse, dolphin, shark, manta ray, whale) Which sea animals have flippers? (dolphin, turtle, walrus, seal)

Sentence knowledge: Help the child to count the number of words in each sentence.

Word knowledge (phonics): Encourage the child to point at the word *see* on any page. Sound out the phonemes in the word: *s-ee*. Ask the child to sound out each letter as they point at it and then blend the sounds together to make the word *see*.

Word recognition: Challenge the child to race you to point at the word *the* on any page.

Rounding off

Sing the following song:
A sailor went to sea, sea, sea
To see what he could see, see, see.
But all that he could see, see, see
Was the bottom of the deep blue sea, sea, sea.

Word coverage

Topic words
butterfly fish
clown fish
cod
dolphin
eel
frogfish
manta ray
octopus
puffer fish
sea
sea snake
seahorse
seal
shark
turtle
walrus
whale

High-frequency words
can
see
the
you

Sentence stem
Can you see the _____?

Ask children to read these words:

cod	p. 5
fish	p. 7
puffer	p. 9
shark	p. 14
eel	p. 16